CABINS

CABINS

Written and Photographed BY

Ralph Kylloe

GIBBS SMITH
TO ENRICH AND INSPIRE HUMANKIND
Salt Lake City | Charleston | Santa Fe | Santa Barbara

First Edition
12 11 10 09 08   5 4 3 2 1

Text and Photographs © 2008 by Ralph Kylloe

Published by
Gibbs Smith
P.O. Box 667
Layton, Utah 84041

Orders 1.800.835.4993
www.gibbs-smith.com

Designed by Pollard Design
Printed and bound in China

Library of Congress Cataloging-in-Publication Data

Kylloe, Ralph R.
  Cabins / written and edited by Ralph Kylloe ; photographs by Ralph
Kylloe.— 1st ed.
      p. cm.
  ISBN-13: 978-1-4236-0370-2
  ISBN-10: 1-4236-0370-2
  1. Vacation homes—United States. 2. Log cabins—United States.
I. Title.
  NA7575.K98 2008
  728.7′20973—dc22
                          2008016108

To
Lindsey

CONTENTS

INTRODUCTION

I've wanted to do a book on waterfront homes for a long time, and this book is indeed a collection of rustic homes that are situated on lakes, rivers or ponds. However, it is difficult to see this in most of the photographs because trees often obstruct views of the water from the houses.

Although for centuries humans lived near water mostly for subsistence purposes, in our day water is piped everywhere and even desert communities thrive, thanks to this precious resource.

Strangely, but conscious of obvious realities, many primitive cultures have purposely avoided waterfront living. Interviews with indigenous peoples in South America and Africa have indicated that although waterfront living has its advantages in terms of transportation, food supplies, fresh water for bathing and cooking, as well as for reasons purely aesthetic, many "tribes" choose to live distinctly away from the waterfront. Insects that live by the trillions near water can literally drive someone crazy, to say nothing of the dangers of deadly diseases transferred by these nasty creatures. Crocodiles, alligators and hippopotamuses have also been known to make the lives of people who ventured into their territory quite miserable. I am reminded of a story of a Peace Corps worker who tried in vain to teach the people of a small African village to swim. Seeing that her students were quite reluctant to enter a local river, the teacher dove in to demonstrate the joys of immersing oneself in cool water. Seeing a village elder, the teacher asked why no one would enter the water. The chief calmly replied that "the crocodiles usually eat us when we swim." The teacher refocused her attention and concentrated on teaching mathematics and writing.

In spite of these dangers, why, then, do people choose to build homes practically "on" the water? Because we love it! And if we can't live near the water, we often vacation by it or swim in pools or purchase inflatable pools that hold only a few gallons of water, and we soak our tired toes in it after a hard day of work. When nothing else is available we'll strip down to our skivvies and make fools of ourselves by squirting the water hose at our kids, spouses and friends—and what fun it is! Besides being fun, water cools us down when we're too hot. It completely takes our minds off any tedium and troubles we may be having.

On a more serious side, although some people will take offense at this, living creatures came from water. We are, in reality, more than 50 percent water ourselves. Alien creatures in an episode of *Star Trek: The Next Generation,* referred to humans as "bags of water." And that we are! It's inside of us and we are a part of it. Water is strange stuff. It offers mystery and folly. It is quite unexplainable in its physical state. It magically loses its form and descends quickly downward, responding to the force and call of gravity. Yet, when it freezes, it responds perfectly to the laws of physics that are the same throughout the entire cosmos. And it can disappear in front of our very noses. Turning into formless gas, it fires the imagination as we watch billowing clouds rumble across the skies. It is the ultimate Rorschach test.

We've been known to ponder the great questions of life on the shores of the great oceans. We sail upon the waters and we swim in it. We consume the very products of the oceans and marvel at the variety and beauty of the life within it. We thrill at its calmness and we marvel at its violence and beauty. The sounds and rhythms of the waters quiet us and remind us of our time spent in the womb of our mothers. We live on a blue planet. We could not and would not exist without water.

At the same time there is tremendous mystery in the water. We thrill and cower as we consider the mysterious entities that dwell in the deep. Its beauties are vast and its dangers are ever present. It both excites us and

frightens us as we contemplate our relationship with water. It is part of us and we belong to it. It offers an unmistakable, unspoken magnetism.

So, with good reason, we create both grand and simple homes on the shores of the water. And if we have not a waterfront home then we either camp near it or live as close as we can to it or bring a man-made fountain into our surroundings to imitate it. Or we spend our vacations splashing in the waves, traveling upon it or diving below it.

The homes we create that allow us to enjoy the water are varied and many. We create forts that guard us and floating platforms that house us. Sometimes we even foolishly build our homes directly in the paths of potential water disasters and humbly pray that they

pass us by. It is a chance, apparently, that we are willing to take. We build homes on grand lakes and on flowing rivers. The closer to the water the better.

Apart from all the romance and worry, we simply love the water. We cherish the memories of carefree youth at summer camp and we revel in the joys of family outings along the shores of the oceans, lakes, ponds, rivers and streams.

I've spent the past thirty years in the rustic design business. Log cabins and all the natural surroundings and furnishings that come with them thrill me. Rustic homes have come a long way in the past few decades. There seems to be a much greater concern for "green" considerations than there was just a few years ago. And along with that, many designers of traditionally built homes are incorporating rustic elements into the their structures. Builders are adding a rustic porch or a rustic den or living room. Designers are adding a piece or two of very high-end rustic furnishings to traditional residential settings.

With these thoughts in mind, out of the hundreds of structures I've seen, I chose a dozen or so homes to include in this book. They represent a broad spectrum of residences, from tiny riverfront cabins to very large family compounds. And to demonstrate innovative rustic styling, I've also included a few modern homes that offer an assortment of rustic architectural elements and high-end rustic furnishings.

As always, there are many people to thank for their help with this book, and I am certain I have inadvertently omitted some who should be mentioned here.

I wish to offer a profound thank-you to the following individuals, including the Steve Byers family, the Carter Bales family, John and Nancy Blangardio, Blake Vincent and family, Paul and Melina Bodor, Randy Holden, Barney and Susan Bellinger, Joe and Peter Pepe, Brian Kelly, Chris Wager, Peter Winter, Eric Gulbrandsen, Lori Toledo, Dan Ryterband and family, Marvin O'Dell, Adam O'Dell, Sally Thurston and family, Todd Klymkom, Jamie Simonds, Jerry Ward and Family, Barbara and Doug Grose, Harry Howard, Nicole Bates, Architect Candace Miller, Norman Van Deist, Dennis Derham, Julia Miller, Keith Anderson, Alyssa Ruffie, Katie Lineberger, Robert and Liz Esperti, Chad Oster, Queen Jackie Spitler, and many others.

I am also deeply indebted to my publisher, Gibbs Smith of Layton, Utah, for his continuing vision and efforts to document and publicize the entire rustic movement. Also I must mention Christopher Robbins, CEO, and my editor, Madge Baird, whose editing and guidance allow me to do what I do. Madge, I personally thank you for your many years of friendship and for not firing me on many occasions when you should have. How you've tolerated me and my occasionally bizarre behavior all these years I'll never know. I'm a better person because of you. Thanks also to architect Larry Pearson of Bozeman, Montana, who has consistently pushed the envelope by designing many of the greatest rustic structures of this century.

My deepest gratitude goes to my wonderful wife, Michele, who tolerates my often-unscheduled absences (and allows me to goof off more than I should), and to my daughter, Lindsey, who often goes with me on photo shoots and competently serves as assistant stylist for many of my photos.

—Ralph Kylloe

THE NORTH CAMP

Some days are easy; others are not. There are some days when I wish that finding a particular home were simple. Most of the homes I photograph are challenging (in a positive sense) to find. The North Camp was one of those places that took a certain amount of effort to locate, especially since the directions read something like "turn left at the big oak tree and be careful when you cross the bridge." Nevertheless, I found the home and was thrilled with the entire setting.

Part of an old family compound, the North Camp was designed by Michael Bird. The home was created on the site of an old lakeside camp that had been torn down. The new building was greatly expanded and included parts of the old original fireplace. This home is actually a guest cabin and serves as living quarters for the owners and guests while the new home is under construction. It offers two thousand square feet of living space and includes two bedrooms, a small kitchenette, living and dining areas, and three bathrooms.

It was built by Jim Frenette of School House Renovations. The building includes cast-iron radiators as well as in-floor radiant heat. The floors are oak, and different types of woods were included in both the interior and exterior of the home. Mason Michael Donah created the living room fireplace, and mason Mike Stender created the bedroom fireplaces. The stones for the fireplaces were actually recovered from an old crib dock on the lake. The doors, cabinets, and kitchen were created by builder Bill Oralgio.

Jim Frenette also built the boathouse. Containing a number of watercraft and accessories, the boathouse offers three wet boat slips and one dry slip for canoes and other small craft. The large electric cruising boat was built by the Elco Electric Launch Company in Athens, New York.

The owners, an astute couple with superb taste, were actively involved in its architecture and the interior design. They appreciate good craftsmanship and spent significant time on details when visiting. The home is furnished with many pieces of rustic furnishings, including items from artist Barney Bellinger of Sampson Bog Studios.

Above:
Painted with pastel colors, these wooden
deck chairs and side tables make a
favorite place for morning coffee.

Right:
The site for this compound is an isolated
lake in the Northeast. The benches in
the foreground are made from cedar.
The boathouse has three boat slips and
a fourth bay to store canoes and other
water toys! It has cedar shingles on the
roof and side, as well as cedar poles on
the exterior walls.

Previous Overleaf:
This home has the classical Adirondack
elements: cedar shake shingles, capped
chimneys, bark-on cedar poles and
triangular windows.

View of the boathouse from a separate dock used for swimming.

Above and Right:
The contemporary boat is by ELCO
Electric. Since it is powered by battery
electricity, it glides silently across
the water without disturbing the
resident loons.

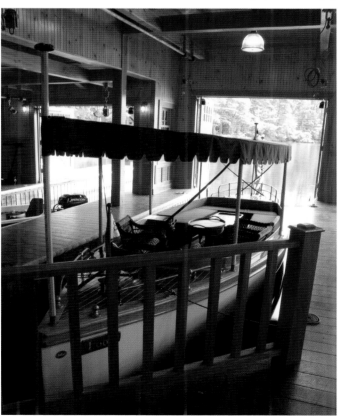

Facing:
The dramatic stump-base sofa table in the foreground was created by rustic artist extraordinaire Barney Bellinger of Sampson Bog Studios. A variety of accessories, including duck decoys, add to the setting.

Above:
Red leather lounge chairs provide comfortable seating in the living room. Because wood often feels monochromatic, red brings needed life to rustic settings.

Left:
This table is complete with a mosiac top and fallow antlers surrounding the base.

Previous Overleaf:
This fireplace was created by mason Michael Donah from stones retrieved from a local crib dock. The mantel was constructed with a cherry tree, complete with a massive cherry burl. The walls are partially covered with horizontal wainscoting.

Right:
A small kitchenette occupies one section of the home. The cabinets were created by Bill Oralgio.

Facing:
This bump-out dining area has built-in seating and hickory chairs. A small antler chandelier lights the room.

A rustic iron wall rack serves as storage for pots, pans and other kitchen utensils.

A small industrial stove sits in the kitchenette corner. The countertops and blacksplash are honed granite.

Facing and Left:
An antique Heriz carpet graces the floor. The cast-iron radiators are completely functional and provide an early-1900s ambiance. The custom cabinet has a unique crown of fallow deer antlers. The lack of curtains allows sunlight to flood the room, while a spectacular view of the lake is ever present.

Left:
An antique Heriz carpet rests under
the bed, making a nice landing for
tootsies at first rise in the morning.

Above:
This extraordinary bed and stump-base
lamp table were created by artist
Barney Bellinger. Bellinger often
adorns his furniture with original
paintings.

Above:
Bellinger also created this high-drama
painting, complete with a frame made
of parts from antique bamboo fly rods.

Right:
The master bedroom has a working
fireplace created by mason Mike
Stender as well as a bump-out with
built-in seating.

Right:
The fireplace in a second bedroom boasts a mantel made from an old hand-hewn barn beam.

Facing:
An antique iron bed is covered with country fabrics. The gable ends of the room are covered with birch bark. Eric Gulbrandsen created the blanket chest at the foot of the bed.

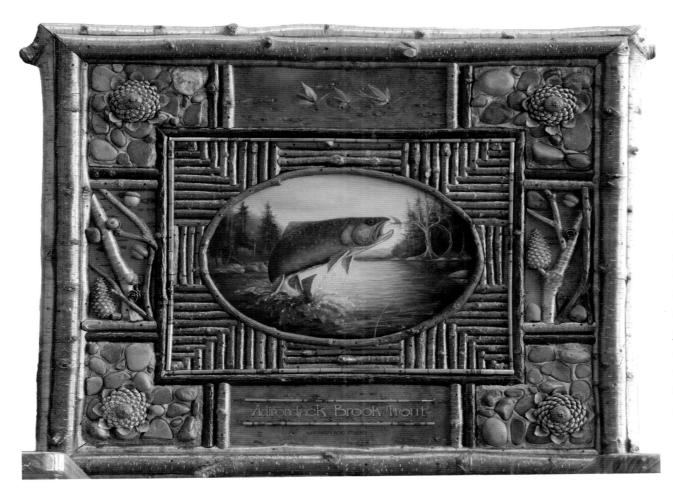

Facing and Left:
These three pieces were created by artist Barney Bellinger. Not only does he create the paintings, but he builds the furniture as well. The frame was created with inlaid stones and pinecones. Half-round twigs were also applied to the frame. Bellinger's artwork is highly sought after and individuals have been known to wait for years to acquire a piece from him.

Bear Rock Lodge

Tucked neatly on a ledge overlooking a glorious body of water sits *Bear Rock Lodge.* The name of the home hints at a bit of mystery and can be interpreted in different ways. The reality is that the home was constructed on a serious rock ledge that contained several caves. Folklore tells us that an old bear lived in one of the caves below the home—hence the name. On the other hand, after excavating the immediate grounds in preparation for construction, it was quite apparent that the property on which the home was to be constructed was nothing more than just "bare rock"! And there you have it!

The size of the home is not apparent until one enters the building through an arched door hand-carved with bears, by artist Jamie Sutliss. The building itself offers just about 6,000 square feet of living space and includes five bedrooms, four and a half bathrooms, a kitchen, living and dining areas, and a finished basement.

The exterior of the home is covered with cedar shake shingles, and the grounds are meticulously maintained by the wizards at Wesley Moody Landscaping. The grounds feature winding, rustic rock and boulder staircases, fire pits perfect for roasting hot dogs and marshmallows, and an extensive array of plants and shrubbery. The large overhanging deck reveals an impressive view of the lake. Architect Andrew Wright created the design and his company constructed the buildings.

The compound also displays a unique boathouse complete with two boat slips and an upstairs recreation/game room. The homeowner served as her own decorator and completed the entire project with great taste and casual yet very elegant styling.

Like many vacation homes, Bear Rock is a family retreat. The owners are an active couple who take full advantage of the surrounding area by hiking, swimming, and involving themselves and their family in a full range of other activities. The two family golden retrievers are constant "sidekicks" and no doubt enjoy their time at camp as well. Along with the family cat, they followed me around throughout the day as I made photos of the home.

Bear Rock Lodge offers a timeless experience that will no doubt bring back priceless memories to the owners and guests as life goes on.

Facing:
A floor-to-ceiling fireplace anchors the
great room. A spindle, bow-arm Morris
chair from the Stickley Company offers
a view of the fireplace and the lake.

Left:
Oversized leather armchairs are a
comfortable place for viewing the
lake. A built-in entertainment center
both houses and hides the electronic
appliances.

Right :
The light-colored wall is an ideal back-
drop for the objets d'art that adorn the
walls. The Morris chair in
the foreground has probably been the
place for many afternoon naps!

Facing:
Eight hickory chairs surround the
English-design dining table, while a
chandelier contributes a touch of
gracefulness.

Left:
Frosted glass in the kitchen cabinet doors enhances the simple country design.

Above:
Hanging lights over the island reflect a pine tree motif. The countertop is polished granite. The chairs are hickory.

Right:
The master bedroom contains a king-size rustic bed made by Steve Chisholm. Large upholstered arm-chairs provide seating.

Facing:
The master bath with tile floor offers a classic claw-foot soaking tub.

Facing and Left:
The recreation room, located on the upper floor of the boathouse, is complete with comfortable furniture and game tables. The spacing between the wall and ceiling boards adds an innovative touch to the setting. The chandeliers are in the Arts and Crafts style.

Facing and Above:
Seating on the enclosed porch includes a
variety of wicker rockers, hickory fur-
niture and an interesting assortment of
side chairs that surround a dining table.
The cat on the couch certainly seems to
be enjoying himself after a hard day of
chasing the local critters!

Right:
Adirondack armchairs surround the
fire pit.

Below:
Peeled cedar is the railing material on
the back deck off the main building.
And what a spectacular view!

Facing:
The boathouse at Bear Rock Lodge
offers not only slips for two boats but
an upstairs family game room complete
with comfortable chairs and games of
all sorts. The lower part of the boat-
house exterior is covered with cedar
shingles. Twig architectural elements
cover the gable ends.

CAMP CEDAR ROCK

The owners of many traditionally constructed homes are today adding rustic architectural elements and rustic furniture to their buildings. And with good reason. Many craftsmen around the country today have elevated their skill level to the realm of the artistic and are creating exceptional pieces of rustic furniture. And these pieces are adding to the rustic ambiance of not only rustic homes but contemporary traditional homes as well. Further, it is often quite easy to both add and incorporate rustic architectural elements into traditionally constructed homes.

Camp Cedar Rock is a classic example of how a traditional home can be enhanced by adding rustic architectural elements, rustic furniture and rustic accessories. Residing on the shores of Lake George in the Adirondack Park, the owners take full advantage of the spring-fed lake and its many amenities.

Built in the early 1980s, this home offers four bedrooms, three baths, living and dining rooms, a kitchen and a large deck area complete with outdoor grills and hot tubs. During the past decade the boathouse was converted from an A-frame building to one with a flat upper deck. Complete with slips for two boats, the boathouse offers further gathering space for friends and family members. It also provides housing for many water-related items, including inner tubes, water skis, and more.

The landscaping around the home adds to the ambiance. Offering neatly trimmed lawns and extensive flowers and shrubbery, the home blends well with the local environment. The original builders of the home wisely let stand several mature trees that today provide both shade and character to the setting.

Facing and Above:
Initially the staircase had traditional spindles. To further "rusticate" the home, Marvin and Adam O'Dell were hired to replace the spindles with elk antlers. A contemporary Adirondack guide boat hangs from the ceiling in the hallway.

Above:
A second-floor view shows another section of the staircase and the guide boat.

Left:
A detailed model of a classic Adirondack home rests on a platform on the staircase landing.

Previous Overleaf:
A lakeside view shows the contemporary styling of the home and the boathouse with upper deck.

Above:
The dining room furniture has an English country influence. A small antler chandelier and antler sconces light the room. The frame for the mirror is covered with twigs and birch bark.

Left:
A game table and stools made from peeled cedar.

Facing:
The living room offers a comfortable selection of oversized upholstered armchairs and ottomans. A classic Bar Harbor wicker armchair and ottoman sit in the corner of the room. The painting of an early steamship was created by Veronica Nemethy.

Facing:
The master bedroom is anchored by a king-size bed made from peeled cedar logs. Wooden venetian blinds cover the window.

Left:
The ornate bureau was created by artist Peter Winter. The mantel clock was constructed by Jerry Farrell.

Below:
A detail photo of the bureau shows the twig work, birch bark and antler pulls.

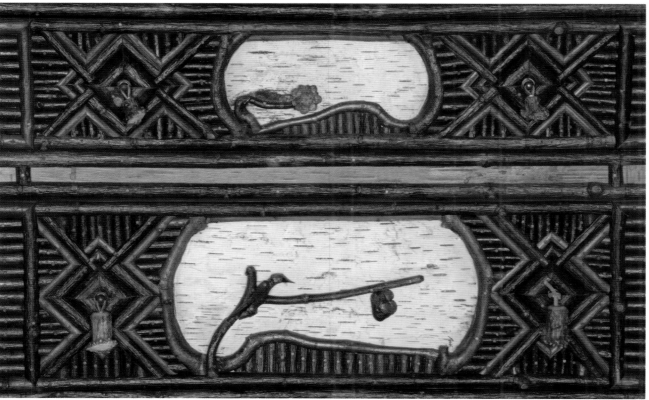

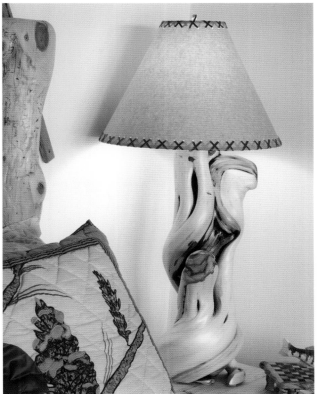

Left:
A second-floor bedroom boasts another peeled-cedar bed. Antique canoe paddles hang from the wall.

Above:
The table lamp is made from twisted juniper.

Above:
A patio-deck has a comfortable teak-wood dining set with canvas umbrella.

Left:
Because the home faces east, hot tub sunrises are a joy to behold!

Facing:
Carefully designed and manicured, the grounds around the home offer a variety of flowering plants that produce an impressive array of colors during their bloom. A pair of outdoor cedar chairs invites visitors to savor the different fragrances of the surrounding plants.

CAMP EDGEMERE

Camp Edgemere is practically impossible to find by car. In fact, it is literally down a goat path of a road that twists and turns for many miles. Driving time from anything quaintly resembling a normal road is more than an hour, and the fastest you can drive on the road to the home is never more than ten miles per hour. And so my first visit was by boat. I met the owners at my gallery a few years ago, and they graciously invited me to see their home while it was under construction. We met in town and traveled by their boat to the site.

As a longtime resident of Lake George, I have spent thousands of hours on the lake, boating, swimming, and making photos, so I was very familiar with the site on which Edgemere was being constructed. I had fished the lagoon many times. It's a magical place. (As a side note, I had also spent quite a bit of time on the site during the annual Audubon bird count held just before Christmas. Because of the location and being the "low man on the totem pole," I was always "awarded" the site and had to walk in many miles through ice and snow to conduct the count. And I was never disappointed. I am one of just a few people who for two years in a row spotted barred owls!)

At any rate, new construction projects always concern me, and it was a disturbing thought to consider the removal of ancient trees and the disruptions of a fragile environment. Nonetheless, as time went by, I had to complement the designers and builders of the home, as it appeared that the buildings were blending nicely with the environment; the large, majestic trees that had stood on the site for many years would continue to enhance the setting.

Designed by architect Roger Bartels, Camp Edgemere is a complex of buildings and can easily be considered a continuation of the Adirondack great camp tradition. Created as a family compound, the facility consists of the main house, three connected guest cabins, a game room over a garage, a boathouse, and several other small rustic structures, including gazebos, gathering huts, and several settings of rustic outdoor furniture. Lincoln Logs provided the timber framework for the home, and John Abrahamson of Abrahamson Masonry completed the stonework.

Facing:
The interior of the home is timber framed. Large pine trees were harvested, dried and assembled to make the framework. Framing by Lincoln Logs. The detail work on the stair railings, created from bark-off cedar, was completed by Phil Kellogg.

Left:
Newel posts for the staircase are in the Arts and Crafts style of the early 1900s. The stairs up to the first landing are granite.

Right:
Iron lanterns and chandeliers through-
out the home reflect both an Austrian
and an Arts and Crafts influence.

Facing and Overleaf:
A large moose head mount overlooks
the entryway. The cozy living room
offers a pair of Arts and Crafts
bow-arm Morris chairs by the Stickley
company. The massive fireplace and
the stonework throughout the com-
pound were completed by John
Abrahamson Masonry.

Right and Facing:
Two further views of the living room reveal leather couches and armchairs covered with kilim carpets from Turkey.

Above:
This sideboard created by Eric Gulbrandsen was made with highly figured flaming birch. The insets on the doors are covered with birch bark.

Right:
Peter Winter crafted the dramatic, original console table.

Facing:
A sitting room off the main living room offers comfortable seating, including two armchairs covered with animal hides.

Facing:
The central dining room, with a rectangular dining table surrounded by six chairs made from birch trees, allows for views of the lake and the surrounding countryside.

Above:
The ultramodern kitchen boasts hi-tech appliances, an island with wet bar and simple barstools made of birch wood. The countertops are Vermont soapstone.

Right:
The design on the kitchen cabinets reflects a Vienna Secessionist influence popular in the early 1900s.

Above and Facing:
Each of the three guest cabins has fire-place and hickory furniture, and is situated for a captivating lake view.

Above:
The dramatic bed made from yellow birch trees was designed and created by Chris Wager. The pastel hanging on the wall was painted by Albert Nemethy.

Right:
The kids' room in the main house offers bunk beds created to fit a full-size mattress on the bottom and a twin mattress on top. The beds were created by Robby Secor.

Facing:
Off the master bedroom, the bathroom has a glass shower and a French-style soaking tub from which one can enjoy a dramatic view of the lake. The floors are southern yellow pine.

Facing:
A game room above the garage has a full fireplace and complete wet bar; the furniture is hickory. The mantel above the fireplace includes an ornate Adirondack wilderness scene created by artist Mike Triveria. The beer shown here was brewed in the Adirondacks by the Coopers Cave Brewing Company.

Above:
This dramatic eight-foot sofa table with root and elk antler base was constructed by Chris Wager.

Right:
The pool table, built in 1905, was artfully restored by Bank Shot Billiards.

Facing:
Wicker furniture and in-floor radiant heating make the enclosed back porch truly an extension of the living space.

Left:
The gazebo was constructed of bark-on cedar in classic Victorian style. The structure was created by the creative folks at Romancing the Woods in Woodstock, New York.

Right:
The outdoor furniture was created by
Romancing the Woods.

Below:
The warming hut offers an in-ground
fire pit perfect for warming cold toes
after a day of ice-skating on the lake.

Far right:
An exterior of view of the warming hut
complete with large logs and slate roof.

A set of six classic Adirondack armchairs sits around a fire pit at the water's edge.

The boathouse has two slips. The roof of the structure is covered with Vermont slate.

Overleaf:
A full view of Camp Edgemere suggests great design and a successful effort to work with the environment.

CHAPEL OF THE ASSUMPTION

Most people would not think of a church as a vacation home. Nonetheless, the owners of this home had great vision and taste when they purchased the Chapel of the Assumption, located on the shores of a great Adirondack lake, in 2005. The building was created in 1921 and served the local community for many years. (I suspect the preacher greatly enjoyed his assignment—especially in the summers.) It is now a vacation home for the owners, and, fortunately, they are able to take frequent advantage of the setting.

Once the building was purchased, contractor Dean Holland, who had attended this Catholic church as a child, was brought in to upgrade it.

The upgrades included leveling the floors; installing new heating, plumbing, and electrical systems; and adding architectural details to the setting. Interestingly enough, the owners felt the huge nine-by-seven-foot original stained glass window did not complement the home, so they located another church that had long admired the window and donated it to them.

The home has five bedrooms and five bathrooms. The property also features a great hot tub and a spectacular boathouse topped off with a sunbathing/lounge deck that offers extraordinary views of the setting sun. The property also includes a complete tiki bar with running water as well as a full bar and a barbeque. Extensive landscaping adds to the rustic ambiance of the home.

The interior home is furnished with a museum-quality collection of rustic furniture and an assortment of antique items.

Left:
The center of this former church is
turned into a living room with a fireplace, tribal carpets, a pair of French
art deco club chairs and a variety of
rustic accessories.

Above:
This ornate armchair was created by
rustic furniture builder Michael
Hutton.

Previous Overleaf:
The entryway to the Chapel of the
Assumption has been modified to
include the rustic screen door with cut-
out pine trees. One of the original
pieces of stained glass remains and adds
not only color but intrigue. The door
on the right leads to the confessional!

Above Left:
This dramatic floor lamp was created by Randy Holden from a yellow birch sapling. The antique rocking chair, circa 1920s, was built by Lee Fountain.

Above Right:
A tripod floor lamp stands next to one of several stained glass windows that were part of the original building.

Below:
The base of the floor lamp retains its original root structure.

A giant moose head guards the knotty-pine room. The wall on which the trophy hangs is covered with commercially available wallpaper created to resemble birch bark.

Left:
Another section of the living area is for dining, complete with table, bow-back Windsor chairs and a collection of rustic accessories. This area is lit with a small elk-antler chandelier.

Above:
Interesting antiques include this water cooler in old original paint as well as a variety of pack baskets and fishing creels.

Right:
An antique cupboard in old paint serves as display space for country collectibles—tinware, pottery and wooden sculptures.

Facing:
The chandelier in the foreground was created from the antlers of fallow deer. The chandelier over the dining table was made from elk antlers.

Facing:
The center of the interior retains its church-like flavor. An altar once stood where the dining table presently resides. A rustic staircase allows access to the second floor and more bedrooms.

Left:
A built-in bar rests under the second-floor balcony, and an antique pool table now sits where church pews once offered comfort to worshipers.

Facing:
A built-in wine rack rests safely under the staircase, while a stuffed cougar guards the spirits!

Left:
Exquisite staircase and window detailing. Twig appliqué was added to the molding above the windows.

Right and Below:
Detail of a cupboard created by
artist Randy Holden. The piece was
created from a variety of soft woods
and hardwoods.

Facing:
The walls are painted a vibrant
yellow. The lower section of some of
the walls has wainscoting.

The antique pool table was created in the late 1890s. The floors are knotty pine.

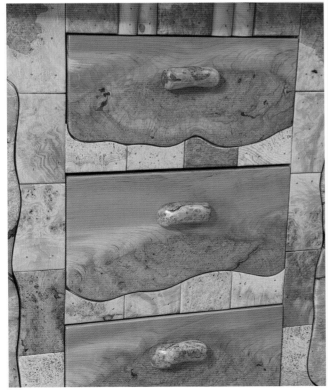

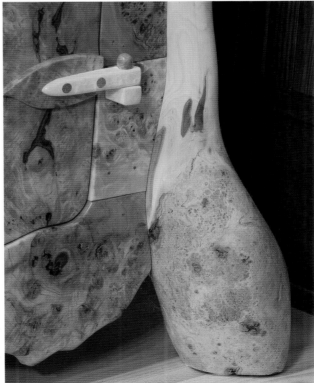

Above and Left:
Steve Chisholm crafted this exceptional cupboard from maple burls. The hinges are handmade.

Facing:
The living room offers comfortable
oversize upholstered furniture and a
variety of accessories.

Left:
An exciting rocking chair by Tim
Duncan is made from redwood and
twisted juniper.

Below:
This stump-base table was created by
Steve Chisholm. The top was created
from maple and the bottom is yellow
birch.

Left:
The kitchen, which was custom made for the building, is more indicative of an English setting than something found in an old church. The setting is masterfully accessorized with colorful dishes and accouterments. The counter-tops are granite.

Above:
Another view of the kitchen shows the tile floor.

Above and Right:
The master bedroom is centered on a
maple burl bed made by Steve
Chisholm. The bedroom not only over-
looks the lake but also offers immediate
access to the outdoor hot tub. A bent
willow lounge chair, complete with
fluffy cushions, occupies a corner of the
bedroom.

Right and Below:
Other bedrooms in the home exude
their own style and ambiance.

One bathroom offers a built-in vanity with doors covered in birch bark. The ornate rustic mirror was constructed by artist Lori Toledo.

Facing:
Seen from the lake, the home is surrounded by towering white pine trees.

Right:
A root settee made in China sits on the
back porch.

Below:
A tiki hut complete with wet bar and
coolers sits near the shore of the lake.

Above:
A rustic twig swing hangs between a pair of mature pine trees.

Left:
Paths and exceptionally maintained landscaping add to the setting.

Right:
A back-porch view of the boathouse deck shows a place to relax on lounge chairs. For a quick wake-up, guests are invited to jump off the end of the boat-house through the gates into the cool water below!

GOLDEN TROUT CAMP

On the shores of the Gallatin River in Montana rests a log cabin that I've stayed in many times. I've caught great trout in the river behind the house, wild bull elk sneaked up on me, and black bears walked up on the porch and nearly put me into cardiac arrest. The cabin itself reflects the taste of an advanced collector who thrills in finding rustic antique treasures and decorating in the rustic style. I featured the cabin in one of my earlier books titled *Adirondack Home*. Later, the owner expanded the compound, adding a small cabin just a few feet from the shoreline of a spring creek that feeds the Gallatin River a hundred yards downstream.

Designed as a studio, the cabin (now known as Golden Trout Camp) was created by Rick Secora with the help of his son, Gus, of Secora Deadwood Creations. Created mostly from 150-year-old reclaimed wood, the cabin was constructed in a yard just south of Bozeman. It was then shipped on a flatbed truck to its present location. Unfortunately, the terrain prevented the truck from getting close enough to the site, so a huge crane was brought in to place the building on its final resting place. And, from what I understand, it was no easy task to "settle" the building. Apparently, seven big men were needed to push the cabin the last few inches, as the crane was in serious jeopardy of toppling over!

The built-in shelves and the window trim were created from materials acquired from a historical stagecoach station. The workbench is actually a twelve-foot-wide, three-inch-thick piece of reclaimed oak. The stonework between the ground and the building was created by Austrian brothers Hans and Franz Schernthaner. The rocks are called Chief Joseph antique stones and are found in the Yellowstone basin.

The cabin is a paragon of comfort and efficiency. It's an ideal place to get away from it all, as there are no phones, computers, or TVs! It's the perfect place to tie flies, write poems, read a book, or write the great American novel. Just be sure to bring your flashlight and make a lot of noise when venturing from the cabin at night. I personally attest that the grizzly and black bears are watching your every move!

Facing:
The historical material used to create
the Golden Trout Camp has warmth,
charm and character. An oversized
lounge chair covered with southwestern
fabric has been the site of many an
afternoon snooze. The blankets and
curtains reflect western motifs.

Left:
A variety of rustic accessories enhance
the ambiance of the cabin.

Right:
Antique lanterns are often electrified
and used as both interior and exterior
lighting. An elk skull rests on top of the
light platform.

Facing:
A classic "Gypsy Chair" made of cedar
rests on the front porch. The porch
banister was constructed from dead
lodgepole pine branches.

HEMLOCK LEDGE

I've been closely associated with Hemlock Ledge for more than thirty years. The historic complex, consisting of a house and accompanying buildings, is an example of American rustic architecture and is considered one of the Adirondack great camps. Designed by architect Julian C. Levy and constructed by Harry Levy, the building was completed in 1906. The home sits on the shores of bucolic Tupper Lake in the Adirondack Mountains of upstate New York.

For years I sold the former owner dozens of high-end pieces of antique rustic furnishings and accessories. Several years ago the owner passed away and, unfortunately, most of the contents were sold. A year or so later, the property was purchased by an astute couple whose vision for the property was both historical and stylistic. Shortly after they purchased the home, the pipes froze during a bitter cold spell, causing significant damage to the building. Fortunately, the home was fully restored, and little by little has regained its subtle grandeur and character..

Down a dusty road in the northern Adirondack Park rests a gate made of peeled cedar trees. An old log sign above the gate announces your arrival at the camp. Following the road to the left, it dead-ends at Hemlock Ledge. The complex contains a main building, a boathouse, a garage, a larger bunkhouse, and a smaller lakefront guest cabin. Another unoccupied historical building is also on the property and is in the process of being refurbished.

For many years, the owners of Hemlock Ledge have fed the birds from several stands and platforms. The chatter of songbirds is ever present. Squirrel and deer take full advantage of the available food. The closely manicured lawn glows green, and the mature white pine and oak trees "whisper and sway" in the dance of the wind.

The lake—miles and miles of it—splashes against the shores and beckons visitors to kick off their shoes and dangle their toes in the cool, clear water. Although it's a large lake, few homes rest on its shores. Nonetheless, classic antique boats are often seen cruising its edges and shallows. And the occasional fisherman can be seen casting lures in hopes of enticing the finned denizens of the deep to sample his offerings. In one of the isolated coves, a large summer camp offers visitors weeks of thrills, companionship, hot dogs and marshmallows, and summertime joy. It's a place where friends are made, character is developed, and swimming skills are honed. Cruising by boat in the evening, you can hear camp songs as well as laughter and giggles of happy campers. The world would be a better place if everyone could share the joys of summers by the lake with friends.

The interior of Hemlock Ledge is less a traditionally furnished rustic camp than one might expect. It reflects the owners' admiration for formal decor as well as their appreciation for quality rustic furniture. The kitchen is an absolute delight, and I must admit that I've had several great dinners there as well as a memorable wild duck feast carefully prepared by a visiting Russian chef and served in style in the grand dining room!

Each room has its own bath, complete with antique sinks and claw-foot bathtubs. My wife and I have enjoyed sleeping in a traditional Japanese bed in one of the bedrooms. We can only smile as we recall being lulled to sleep by the lapping waves and a hooting great horned owl that, no doubt, terrorizes the birds and squirrels on his nightly raids. Hemlock Ledge is a quiet place—a place for reflection and companionship. That's why it's called a great camp!

Facing:
The low ceilings in the living room help the fire keep the room cozy warm. The building has an Arts and Crafts feel of the very early 1900s. The inscription over the fireplace reads, "The ornament of a house is the guest who doth frequent it."

Left:
The handmade metalwork, including the six-foot torchiers, is indicative of the period in which the home was constructed.

Above:
The small octagon table resting between two period armchairs in the study was created by Chris Wager.

Right:
In the living room are a pair of hickory sofas in colorful fabric. The sofa table, with paddles and original painting, was created by Barney Bellinger. The wood floors and walls have mellowed to a rich golden brown.

Facing:
Resting next to the living room fireplace is this spectacular cabinet. Probably originally a "hunt board" in Switzerland, the piece was made from Linden wood sometime between the 1890s and 1930s. It serves here as a liquor cabinet and storage unit.

Left:
An original bear hall tree sits at the entrance to the dining room. Commonly referred to as "Black Forest," the pieces were actually made in Berne, Switzerland, beginning in the late 1890s and into the 1930s. The pieces were made of Linden wood and created for the tourist trade in Switzerland.

Far left:
The dining room offers an extraordinary 1930s dining set made in the Chippendale style. The room also offers a full working fireplace.

Above:
A round service table made of mahogany rests in an alcove surrounded by built-in seating.

Left:
A walk-in pantry offers plenty of storage space for an extensive collection of dinnerware.

Facing:
In classical Adirondack fashion, most of the walls in the home are covered with pine wainscoting. The kitchen at Hemlock Ledge has been upgraded to include industrial appliances. Regardless, it retains its historical camplike ambiance and simplicity.

Above left:
A large antique sideboard made of ash and chestnut sits in a corner of the kitchen.

Above right:
Built-in cabinets are found throughout the home.

Left:
The home also contains an elaborate fire suppression system. Charming in their own way, the hose and storage bracket are original to the home.

Above:
A Barney Bellinger bureau blends with
the setting in the master bedroom.

Right:
The master bedroom offers this king-
size bed created by Unique Woodworks.
The small bedside cabinet was custom
made by Chris Wager.

Left:
This pair of queen-size beds occupies
one of three guest bedrooms. The beds
were masterfully created by rustic artist
Brian Kelly, constructed of kiln-dried
yellow birch trees.

Above:
A small bathroom off the guest room
offers a single pedestal sink and claw-
foot bathtub.

Above:
A game room in the top floor of the boathouse is complete with pool table, canoe shelves, and a stunning root chair created by Jerry Farrell.

Left:
The second-floor boathouse balcony offers an excellent view of the lake.

Facing:
The boathouse has slips for two boats below and a game room upstairs. A small sand beach adjacent to the boathouse has seen its fair share of vacationers.

SKYE NOTCH

Skye Notch is not a normal place. Finding it requires advanced degrees and significant experience in orienteering. It's located an hour or so off a main highway, and it's best to slow down to avoid ruining your vehicle on the copious potholes and frost heaves that plague the road in spring. It's also best to slow down to avoid hitting any of the many deer that seem to jump in front of your vehicle at every turn. Eventually, a small road sign signals a right turn and you think you've arrived. But it's many more miles of back-country roads and turns that wind through the landscape like the veins in your hands.

Eventually, if you have patience and are good at following directions, you'll come to an obscure wooden gate that you'll have to open if you're on the list of invited guests. And even when you're inside the compound, it's not apparent that you've arrived.

Finally, the scenery unfolds before you. First are several mature hardwood trees. Beyond the trees are mountains and vast acres of wilderness. In the valley below sits a gorgeous pond that was the dream of the owner. He placed hundreds of rainbow trout in the pond with the intent of creating a private fly-fishing sanctuary. Unfortunately, the local wildlife had other ideas. The otters eventually won out as they succeeded in defeating fences and other methods of limiting access to the water. Nonetheless, in time the owners realized their limits and resigned themselves to sitting on their porch and watching the otters climb through the fences and enter the pond in both summer and winter. And, of course, every time an animal descended into the water, it returned with a fresh trout, which was consumed on the spot!

Nonetheless, the home itself remains a bastion of creativity and innovation. Furnishings were acquired from not only the Adirondacks but Europe and the Far East as well. Large European armoires were installed in place of built-in closets. Historical European architectural elements were installed as doors, railings, and for other uses.

Furnishings covered with intricate tapestries occupy several of the rooms, and oriental carpets cover much of the exposed floor space in the home. Advanced collections of artwork, including several original bronze busts, occupy wall and gallery space in the home. Antique tubs and fixtures grace many of the bathrooms, and an antique copper fixture doubles as a beer tap in the poolroom.

The custom kitchen is a model of efficiency and design, offering little resemblance to what one might expect in a log cabin. The living room features a single three-story-high stone that has been plumbed for a running stream and chiseled to make room for a fireplace.

The basement houses a hideaway wine cellar with an advanced collection of wines, and down a few more hallways is a family entertainment room complete with leather reclining chairs for comfortable movie viewing.

The home was built by Maple Island Homes in Michigan. Various architects offered their design ideas, but the home really is the creation of the owners. I've enjoyed every minute I've spent there!

Above:
The second-floor balcony offers views of
the pond and the surrounding moun-
tains. The banisters and railing systems
were made from peeled cedar.

Left:
Antlers from red stag, moose and fallow
deer were integrated into the railing sys-
tem on the staircase. Ed Figueroa con-
structed it.

Facing:
The main entrance to the home sits
under the portico. The front entry
doors were imported from Europe. A
massive iron chandelier includes oak
leaf, pinecone, bear and flower motifs.

Facing:
The soaring trees extending from the pillars were added by artist Ed Figueroa after the building was completed. Figueroa also created the balcony railing from antique European architectural elements.

Left:
Obviously the focal point of the room, the "rock," as it's affectionately called, not only serves as a fireplace but also contains a waterfall and stream system! The fixture stands thirty-two feet tall.

Previous Overleaf:
The living room, quite large in scale, has numerous seating areas. The furnishing of the home reflects the superb taste and individuality of the owners. Enhanced by sophisticated and often exotic textiles, the room takes on an elegant dimension. An original Chinese opium bed (right background) offers another dimension to the setting.

The side table with tiger maple top was made by Chris Wager. Fabrics and textures used on the furnishings bring a smile to all who encounter them!

This antique tall case clock was found in Sweden and presently rests under the eaves of the balcony in the main living room.

Facing:
The game room is personally my
favorite room in the house. The historical cabinetry was imported from
Europe. The large copper kettle was
modified to become a dispenser of local
brews! The pool table is in frequent use.

Above and Left:
Ornate fabrics cover the upholstered
furniture throughout the home. Not of
a style normally seen in log homes, the
furniture and textiles represent an
innovation in rustic style and design.

Right :
The complete kitchen was designed by the owners of Skye Notch and constructed in Italy! The island countertop is polished granite. The chandelier over the island was custom made.

Facing:
A fanciful iron chandelier overhangs the dining table. The kitchen fireplace reflects historical design.

Facing:
This European bed, covered in classic textiles and pillows, provides guests a very comfortable rest, as well as a view of the countryside when the sun rises.

Left:
One of the many bathrooms is fitted with this classic Victorian case piece that has been modified into a vanity.

Right:
Antique European architectural elements were incorporated into many facets of the home. This large hall mirror now stands proudly over the bedroom fireplace.

Below and Facing:
A private sitting room next to the game room offers comfortable seating and accessories. The bookcases were found in Europe and incorporated into the setting.

Facing:
Wandering down a winding staircase, visitors arrive at the wine cellar that is situated directly under the fireplace. Old beams and antique furniture create an old-world ambiance for a fine collection of beverages!

Left:
An exceptional entertainment center, complete with popcorn machine and reclining leather armchairs, is conveniently located right next to the wine cellar.

360 RANCH

It was a gorgeous fall day, and literally hundreds of deer chomped on the late-season grasses spread over the prairies we passed. Counting their numbers was out of the question. Occasionally a few antelope popped into view. The region, just north of Yellowstone National Park, had a pack of wolves that occasionally howled in the darkness of night. Black bears and an occasional grizzly wandered the area: during my visit, the local paper carried a story of an aggressive bear attacking hunters just a few miles from the project. I chose to stay out of the woods to avoid both caffeine-happy hunters and aggressive bears.

Mature cottonwood trees presented their radiant colors and occasionally shed a few leaves, reminding me of the ever-changing seasons of life. (At sixty years old, I seem to have a semiconscious persistent thought that life does not go on forever.)

Having visited this area for many years and fished every corner of the local rivers and streams, I was familiar with the regional architecture and the local environment. The setting that slowly appeared before me was nothing less than a thrill to behold. It reminded me of all the good things in life.

After entering a gate, we progressed slowly down a rutted dirt road. Around a sharp corner, a gorgeous building complete with aged beams appeared before us. "Oh, that's only the caretaker's house," my guide mentioned. "The main house is a bit farther down the road. Just keep going." I would have been perfectly satisfied with the house at hand. Around a bend, we crossed a bridge that traversed a small trout stream. Another meadow with tall grasses opened up. Farther down the road we came to an unusual symmetrical cabin tucked neatly in a gully (more technically referred to as a bench); there was a half-acre pond in the backyard. I struggled to acknowledge that this was just a guest cabin, upon learning that the large main home would be located near the stream and other buildings such as a horse barn would be placed throughout the property in the coming years.

Nonetheless, the owners also wanted a guesthouse for their adult children. Architect Candace Miller of Livingston, Montana, worked with the owners to carefully and thoughtfully plan the site. Garret Jasinski from Yellowstone Traditions served as project superintendent during construction. Ed Matos of Bridger Engineering served as engineer. The interiors were provided by Haven of Bozeman, Montana.

The result is a duplex with individual porches on the back to accommodate individual families and guests, thus ensuring some seclusion. All in all, this is a rather astonishing guesthouse that should knock the socks off anyone invited to spend the night!

Far Left:

Designed as a duplex, the structure offers two completely different living quarters so guests can have some privacy. Separate porches overlooking the lake are on opposite ends of the building.

Left above:

A steel bridge made by the Rosco Steel Company allows access to the property.

Left below:

The building exterior is rendered more interesting by different patterns inlaid into the walls. The diamond pattern is a classical example of Adirondack design.

Right:
The home was built by the creative people at Yellowstone Traditions. Custom hardware, including door hinges and knockers, was created by blacksmith Bill Moore of Big Timber, Montana.

Facing:
Masonry was completed by Brett Evje. The stone used in the building is called Montana moss rock.

Left and Above:

As in many rustic kitchens today, the refrigerator is hidden behind antique barn board. The countertops are soapstone. The iron hood over the range is custom made, and the island is faced with half-round branches from dead-standing lodgepole pine. Recycled barn boards were turned into a custom cabinet with interior lighting. Flooring was also created from reclaimed boards.

Right:
This freestanding display case was created by the cabinet builders at Yellowstone Traditions. The small twigs applied to the piece are the branches of lodgepole pine trees.

Facing:
Hallways create a sense of personal space, as one can disappear into a private room. The white material between the logs is commonly referred to as chinking. Most chinking material used today has the ability to expand and contract, depending on the humidity and weather.

Facing:
The interior styling is by Haven of Bozeman, Montana. The layering of pillows and other textiles adds depth to the room, while subtle window treatments complement the setting.

Left:
This bedroom fireplace was created from locally quarried Montana moss rock. The mantel is granite.

Above:
Bathroom countertops were created
from recycled barn beams.

Right:
Draw blinds cover the bathtub
windows when needed. The tub
surround is a mosaic of small tiles.

Right:
Another bathroom offers a
tub/shower decorated with a
herringbone pattern of tiles.

Facing:
A second guest bedroom has a full
fireplace, comfortable chairs, a desk
area and a queen bed complete with
colorful textiles.

Facing:
A kids' room features built-in bunk beds and direct access to the back porch and lake.

Left:
The walls in the guest powder room are covered with pages from vintage outdoors magazines. This unique innovation makes for interesting reading while getting ready for the day!

Each wing of the home boasts not only a back porch but a private sleeping porch as well.

Above:

The geometric lines of the bed cover-
ings mimic the patterns inherent in
the log walls. This platform bed offers
drawer space below the mattress for
hideaway storage.

Right:

The geometric form of the ceiling fixture complements the linear forms of
the logs. The fixture is lined with
amber mica.

Left:
The back porch (one on each end of the house) is occupied with different styles of rustic furniture. Electrified antique lanterns light the exterior of the home.

Above:
The color and pattern of the textiles blend well with the fall colors.

ROCK LEDGE

Rock Ledge is a family home and a traditional summer family camp. Every time I've been at the site, there have been at least a half dozen kids there plus a few dogs. And all of them have been swimming, playing on the porch, or doing what kids and animals do. It's a very pleasant place to be. The owner of the home eagerly anticipates the weekends and an escape from the craziness of investment banking in Manhattan. He looks forward to a glass of wine and a cigar on his porch overlooking the lake.

There is no TV in this home. People here spend their time playing in the water, putting puzzles together, singing around campfires, and watching the wildlife. Communication amongst family members is both encouraged and intense. It's an old-fashioned place where people get to know each other. For lack of better nomenclature, it's a happy place!

Rock Ledge is perhaps the most casual of the homes I've seen in a while. It is as unpretentious as it is comfortable. It's okay to put your feet up on the coffee table, and it's okay to linger in the kitchen over a cup of coffee, and it's okay to have a drink on the porch overlooking the lake at any hour of the day. Breakfasts have been known to last for hours and often include a dozen or more family members.

The present owners rented the camp for sixteen years before it came up for sale and they bought it! Built in 1945, the home has been maintained and upgraded on several occasions to meet the needs of a growing family and friendly neighborhood kids. But it is the intent of the family to keep the charm and character exactly as it was in the mid-1940s. Presently, the exterior is covered with what is known as "wavy board," "pig pen," or "Adirondack siding." Bark-on Adirondack trimming has been added to the porches and on other areas of the exterior. The interior of the building offers knotty pine walls and plasterboard in a few of the bedrooms. The home also features the original fireplace, which has withstood the test of time.

The owners, a fun-loving couple, have decorated the home with an eclectic collection of rustic beds in all the bedrooms and comfortable furniture throughout the home. The kitchen remains exactly as it was back in 1945, including the original furniture. The living room has oversized, comfortable lounge chairs and a few antique pieces of hickory furniture, as well as oriental carpets.

The porch faces east and guests have been known to enjoy breakfast and the sunrise at the same time. It's a comfortable place that seems to be a timeless statement about lakeside living. I've personally enjoyed every second I've spent there!

Facing:
Built in 1945, the building retains its original character. A large glass chandelier in the form of an acorn adorns the center of the living room. Antique hickory chairs, leather couches and rustic antiques and accessories complement the room.

Left:
The original appliances and dining set from 1945 are still in use at the camp. The venetian blinds that were installed when the home was built are still in use.

Facing:
The massive king-size bed made from yellow birch bark trees is a great place to read books to the kids in the master bedroom.

Right:
Deck chairs on the dock provide a place to gaze at the sunrise and watch the loons float by.

Below:
A set of Amish rocking chairs seem to be occupied at all hours of the day.

SUNSET PINES

Down a winding road, through rolling hills and past farms and tall trees lies a small sign marking a left turn down a two-track dirt road. (Believe me, it's hard to find.) A few turns later, one enters what at first glance appears to be just another contemporary home that rests on the shores of a lake in the northern stretches of America.

Many homes being built in rustic settings today begin with traditional ideas and traditional plans. Property is purchased and homes are designed and constructed. But somewhere along the line, owners realize the inherent beauty and uniqueness of rustic furnishings. And once their home is complete, they add rustic furnishings and a few rustic architectural elements to augment their otherwise traditional home. Such was the case with Sunset Pines.

Sunset Pines offers nearly 3,000 square feet of floor space and includes four bedrooms, four baths, an office, a kitchen, and living and dining rooms. It also features a great deck from which to enjoy the setting sun, complete with outdoor furniture and cooking grill. Carefully landscaped—which was no easy task, considering the sloping land on the lake side of the building—the home also has a docking system to house boats and water toys that are enjoyed by the young owners and their family.

Left:
The leather sofa has back cushions with moose-hide upholstery. The home is comfortable with in-floor radiant heat.

Above:
The armchair was created by artist Barry Gregson, who is widely regarded as the most accomplished rustic chair builder in the country.

Previous Overleaf:
The living room at Sunset Pines has an eclectic array of furnishings, including both traditional and rustic pieces. A fox rests on the fireplace mantel. Of interest are the valances over the sliding doors and windows. The tables were created by Chris Wager, and the rustic armchair was made by Barry Gregson.

Right:
Eric Gulbrandsen created this spectacular cabinet. Eric is known for using highly figured woods in his creations.

Facing:
These dining room chairs were made by Barry Gregson. The corner cupboard and dining room table were created by Gulbrandsen, who often applies a "beaver chew" edge to his tables.

The master bedroom is complete with a yellow birch bed, rustic side tables and rustic valances over the windows.

Above and Left:
The innovative six-drawer chest, tall corner cabinet and mirror were made by Eric Gulbrandsen. The dimensional wood material is highly figured flaming birch. The side chair was made by Barry Gregson.

SWITCHBACK RANCH

We met at 6 a.m. for coffee in Bozeman, Montana. It was still very dark. I was with architect Larry Pearson and Dennis Derham, also from Larry's office. It was very late fall and the early morning drive through Yellowstone National Park was nothing less than glorious. Ice was on the roads but the early morning hues from the rays of the sun lent a sense of awe and mystique to the day. Animals—bison, elk and deer—were everywhere. At one point we had to quickly accelerate our vehicle to avoid being rammed by an irate bull bison that seemed to not appreciate our stares at him.

Dennis, who had lived just outside Yellowstone beyond Cooke City for nine years as a young man, gave us running commentary on the terrain, the local personalities, the architecture, and the fishing and hunting in the area. We had breakfast in a seedy place in Cooke City. The waiter/chef was less than friendly and seemed tired of visitors. We also stopped by a local ranch and endured the ire of the cowboy whose sole purpose in life was to make visitors feel both miserable and unwelcome. And initially, he was quite successful at his job.

But because Dennis had lived on the ranch some twenty years earlier, the ice was broken when the cowboy realized that he and Dennis had several mutual friends.

After we left the ranch we drove for another hour through the southern end of the Beartooth Mountains. In time we found a chained gate that we were supposed to have the lock combination for but did not. So without further discussion we unloaded our gear and climbed the old boot-jack fence and started down the trail. But I have to be honest here. There had been three very serious grizzly bear attacks in the area that week and bears had been known to wander the very trail we were on! So I can clearly say that I was thrilled to see the ranch hand's truck coming to pick us up some twenty minutes into our hike! His first words were, "You were supposed to be here an hour ago." Of course, we apolo-

gized as we loaded our gear into the back of the truck. I, being the low man on the totem pole, of course, rode in the truck bed along with the cow feed, saddles, and other ranch gear.

The ride to the ranch was memorable. We descended at least two thousand feet into a valley on a dirt road covered with boulders that had fallen from the mountaintops. And the driver of the truck, completely confident in his abilities to navigate the goat path, seemed to enjoy scaring the bejesus out of me by aggressively descending to the valley below.

Nonetheless, the setting was nothing less than spectacular! First, a huge field opened up, then we crossed a bridge that transcended the Clark's Fork of the Yellowstone River. More fields followed, then a home and barn of logs, horses and finally the small riverfront cabin we had come to photograph.

Designed by Larry Pearson and constructed by the creative folks of OSM, the project and process were significantly different from what us normal folks think when considering the construction of a home. Peter Belschwender of OSM offered several necessary design and construction solutions to the project. Although small—the home was originally restacked and constructed in the OSM construction yard by log artist Gabe Williams in about six weeks—the problem was how to get the building to a site accessible only by a road that would

terrify even the most experienced Himalayan
Sherpa guides.

With great care, the home was dismantled, driven
to the access road and brought in piece by piece via
helicopter! The entire home was reconstructed on
the site in just forty days! Because the home was on
a river whose waters rose each spring, the building
was placed on a helical pier foundation sunk some
forty feet into the ground. The building is a true
historical, restacked log home and the trusses are
load bearing.

Throughout the day Larry and Dennis served with
honor as my photo assistants and stylists. Several of
the photos presented here include glasses of wine
and wine bottles! The four of us felt it was the ultimate indignity and disrespectful to discard the contents of the bottles, so during the photo shoot at
least several containers of the great grape elixir were
consumed and I am very happy to say that all of the
images I made that day were correctly exposed and
in focus! To make the day even more enjoyable,
ranch hand Darwin Emmitt, a classic cowboy who
feared nothing and could solve every problem, provided us with an endless array of fascinating stories
and local folklore.

The ride home was magnificent as the jutted peaks,
endless rolling hills, forests and animals enhanced
the day.

Above:
Artistically created and well balanced, the room and its furnishings blend together to create an inviting setting. The cabinet on the right has exhibition space for a number of collectibles. A pair of antler table lamps lights the back wall.

Right:
An iron chandelier lights the room while an elk mount stands watch.

Previous Overleaf:
As innovative as it is real, the ranch offers a fresh look in the world of rustic cabins. A pair of even-arm settles provides seating in the living room. A wood-burning stove provides heat and a variety of antique framed artworks grace the walls. A tattered Ganado Navajo carpet adds a lived-in, unpretentious, comfortable feel to the setting.

Antler table lamps rest on a wicker sofa table next to a Victorian walnut sewing chair. The trusses were created from recycled, hand-hewn barn beams.

Facing:
An armchair, surrounded by artwork, rests up against the reclaimed walls.

Left:
The second building is primarily a feasting station. Decorated with country furniture, a great deal of which is covered in old paint, the room begs visitors to relax and stay for a while.

Right and Facing:
Opposite ends of the same room are
presented here. The dining table is sur-
rounded by an assortment of Windsor
chairs. A moose skull with intact
antlers hangs on one end of the room,
while a skull with mountain goat horns
hangs on the opposite end.

Facing:
An antique shelving unit acts as both
a storage and display unit for country
collectibles.

Left:
A wood-burning stove is a reliable heat
source, as long as someone has remem-
bered to chop wood!

Facing:
An antique sink isn't only for washing up in the morning but for washing the dishes as well.

Left:
The shower is located on the outside of the building and is a great place to freshen up—if you don't mind a hundred cows staring at you!

A breezeway connecting the two buildings makes a very nice setting to enjoy an afternoon meal. The table is surrounded by a great collection of snowshoe armchairs.

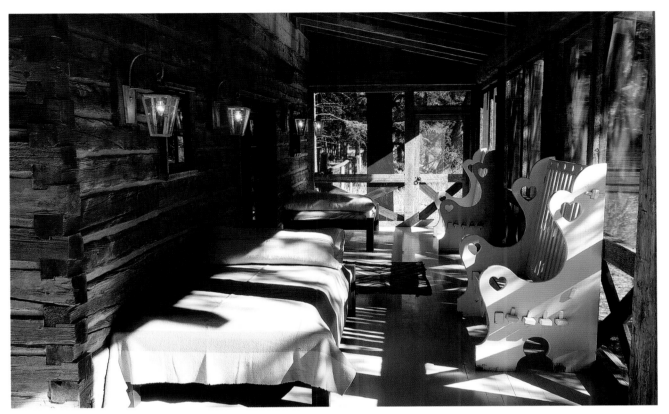

Above:
Another section of the breezeway
doubles as sleeping quarters and a place
to relax on a pair of painted benches.

Left:
Stone slabs serve as stairs to the entryway. Although completely refurbished,
the building retains its historic appeal.

Above:
Artist extraordinaire Dennis Derham of the office of architect Larry Pearson tries his hand at fly-fishing in the river immediately out the back door!

Left:
Gnarly rustic chairs made from fallen timbers provide seating to ponder the great mysteries of life along the banks of the river.

Facing:
The cabin rests in a valley surrounded by two-thousand-foot cliffs.

R ESOURCES

Interior Designers

Barbara Collum
6976 Colonial Dr.
Fayetteville, NY 13066
315.446.4739

Carole Sisson Designs, ASID
117 E. Main Street
Bozeman, MT 59715
406.587.2600

Diana Beattie Interiors
1136 Fifth Ave.
New York, NY 10128
212.722.6226

Halcyon House
802 Avenue of the Americas, Ste.
102
New York, NY 10001
212.920.5177

Haven Interiors
Debra Schull
1001 West Oak Street, Ste. 110
Bozeman, MT 59715
406.522.4188

Hilary Heminway
140 Briar Patch Road
Stonington, CT 06378
860.535.3110

Lohr Design
Chip Kalleen
201 N Illinois Street, Ste. 1720
Indianapolis, IN 46204
317.237.5610

Peace Design
349 Peachtree Hills Ave. NE C2
Atlanta, GA 30305
404.237.8681

Pearson Design Group, Inc.
(PDG)
Architects & Interior Design
P.O. Box 3666
Bozeman, MT 59715
406.587.1997

WISE Associates
Heidi Weiskopf
3150 N. Pima Road #1E
Scottsdale, AZ   85255
602.625.9832

Architects

Michael Bird
77 Riverside Dr.
Saranac Lake, NY 12983
518.891.5224

Kipp Halvorsen
1425 West Main St., Ste. A
Bozeman, MT 59715
406.587.1204

Dan Joseph
P.O. Box 4505
Bozeman, MT 59772
800.800.3935

Miller Architects PC
Candace Tillotson-Miller, AIA
P.O. Box 470
Livingston, MT 59047
406.222.7057

Pearson Design Group, Inc.
(PDG)
P.O. Box 3666
Bozeman, MT 59715
406.587.1997

Prairie Wind Architecture
Jeff Shelden, AIA
206 West Blvd.
P.O. Box 626
Lewistown, MT 59457
406.538.2201

Jeff Thompson
220 S. Ninth Ave.
Bozeman, MT 59715
406.586.3553

Urban Design Group
Peter Dominick
1621–18th St., Ste 200
Denver, CO 80802
303.292.3388

Home Builders
Chris Lohss Construction
P.O. Box 556
Gallatin Gateway, MT 59730
406.763.9081

John Abrahamson Masonry
199 Street Rd.
Argyle, NY 12809
518.638.8051

OSM
417 W. Mendenhall
Bozeman, MT 59715
406.586.1500

School House Renovations
5 High St.
Tupper Lake, NY 12986

Yellowstone Traditions
P.O. Box 1933
Bozeman, MT 59771
406.587.0968

**Rustic Furniture and Design
Galleries**
Black Bass Antiques
P.O. Box 788
Main Street
Bolton Landing, NY 12814
518.644.2389

Fighting Bear Antiques
P.O. Box 3790
375 South Cache Dr.
Jackson, WY 83001
307.733.2669

High Country Designs
P.O. Box 5656
720 Main St.
Frisco, CO 80443
970.668.0107

Ralph Kylloe Gallery
P.O. Box 669
Lake George, NY 12845
518.696.4100

Ross Bros. Gallery
28 N. Maple St.
Florence, MA 01062
413.586.3875

Chocolay River Trading Company
Pam Gilmore
2210 US 41 South
Marquette, MI 49855
906.249.2782

**Places to See and Buy
Great Rustic Stuff**
Adirondack Mountains Antiques Show
Indian Lake, NY

Rustic Furniture Fair
Adirondack Museum
Blue Mountain Lake, NY

Lakeside Living Expo
East Greenbush, NY

Lake, Home and Cabin Show
Minneapolis, MN

Western Design Conference
Jackson, WY

Cowboy High Style
Cody, WY